LIVING THINGS

A simple introduction

Marit Claridge

Illustrated by John Shackell

Designed by Anne Sharples

Consultant: Gillian Ghate

CONTENTS

What is biology?

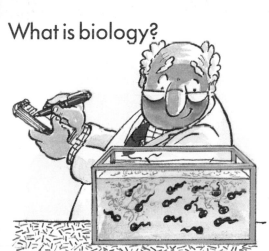

Biology is the study of nature and all living things. Biologists are interested in how the bodies of plants, animals and human beings work, and the way they live.

Biologists ask questions about plants and animals and then try to work out the answers. You can do this too. There are lots of simple tests and experiments you can try to find out more about living things around you.

Some biology experiments can take a long time, so you need to be very patient. If an experiment does not work the first time, try doing it again.

Start a biology scrapbook

Write up your experiments in a scrapbook. Draw what happens at each stage, and note how long it takes.

You will find most of the things you need for the experiments in your home.

Using your eyes

You can learn a lot about living things by watching carefully. Look for living things wherever you go — they may be difficult to spot.

You don't need to buy expensive equipment, but a magnifying glass is very useful for looking close-up at things.

Try to sketch the things you see where they live rather than killing them by bringing them home.

Sunlight and air

Do plants need sunlight?

All living things need energy to live. Green plants can use sunlight to produce the energy they need.

Leaves are green because they contain green colouring matter called chlorophyll. Chlorophyll soaks up energy from the sunlight.

A gas in the air, called carbon dioxide, enters leaves through tiny holes. It mixes with water which has been drawn up by the roots. Sunlight changes the mixture of carbon dioxide and water into sugar and starch, and oxygen, another gas, is given off into the air. This process is called photosynthesis.

Oxygen makers

If you put a jar of pond weed in the sun, you will see lots of bubbles rise in the water. These are bubbles of oxygen.

POND WEED

Buy pond weed in a pet shop.

Do plants breathe?

Try this test to find out whether plants breathe.

Soak two beans for 3 to 4 days.

Put some wet cotton balls or paper towels in a jar and place the beans on top.

Water the jar each day and when the beans have grown roots and shoots, tighten the lid on the jar. Put the jar in a dark place for two days.

Light a long, thin, dry stick and put it into the jar.

The flame goes out. Things need oxygen to burn and this test shows that there is very little oxygen in the jar or the flame would stay alight.

The beans use up the oxygen in the jar and give off carbon dioxide, which shows that they do breathe.

Balancing the air

All animals, including you, have to breathe to live. When we breathe in, our bodies use the oxygen in the air and make carbon dioxide which we breathe out. During the day, plants help to replace the oxygen by photosynthesis.

Fires also use up oxygen.

Some scientists believe that if all the world's forests were cut down, all the oxygen in the air would eventually be used up.

Does sunlight make leaves green?

Sprinkle watercress seeds into two dishes lined with damp paper towels. Put one dish in a light place and the other in a dark cupboard.

Keep the soil damp using a fine spray.

After 3 or 4 days the seedlings growing in the light will be green and healthy, but those in the dark will be yellow.

The seedlings which grew in the dark cupboard will also be taller because they grow upwards to find light.

Sunworshippers

Plants grow to catch as much sunlight as possible. Watch what happens to potted plants on a sunny windowsill.

The leaves turn to face the light.

The heads of sunflowers turn to face the sun and follow its path through the day.

The flower itself cannot photosynthesize, but when the leaves turn to face the sun, the head turns too.

What happens if you turn the plant round?

The chlorophyll in leaves is made by a reaction with the sunlight. Without the chlorophyll the leaves would be yellow.

Which part of the plant is sensitive to light?

Try this test to find out. Plant some oat seeds in two separate dishes and wait for them to grow.

When they are about 1" high, cover the tips of the seedlings in one of the dishes with tiny aluminium foil caps. Place both of the dishes near a window and wait to see what happens.

The covered seedlings will grow up straight and the seedlings without caps bend towards the light. This shows it is the tips of the seedlings that are sensitive to light.

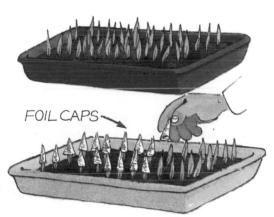

FOIL CAPS

WITHOUT CAPS

WITH CAPS

7

Soil – animal, vegetable or mineral?

Soil may just look like mud but it is made up of many different things. Dig up some soil from under a bush to see what it is made of. Put it in a jar with water, stir it and leave it to settle for a day.

It will fall into separate layers.

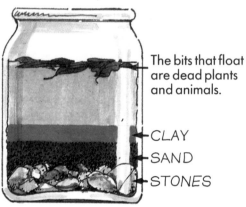

The bits that float are dead plants and animals.

CLAY
SAND
STONES

The stones, sand and clay come from rock which has been worn down by wind and water over millions of years. This is called weathering.

Rot and decay

Dead plants and animals rot and become part of the soil. Rotting is caused by bacteria and fungi which grow on the dead bodies. They break the bodies down into minerals. Other minerals in soil come from weathered rocks.

Worm gardeners

Bristles on its body grip in the soil and make it hard for a bird to pull it out.

They expell fine soil which is good for plant roots.

They pull down leaves from the surface to eat, which then rot in the soil.

They bring up minerals from lower down in the soil.

Their tunnels let in air and water.

Big stones sink as the worms burrow through the soil beneath them.

Worms eat the rotting plants in the soil. As they eat their way through the soil, they improve it for plants in several ways.

A wormery jar

Gently dig over a patch of soil – you will soon come across some worms.

Fill a jar with layers of damp sand and soil and put leaves on top. Add two worms. Cover the jar with dark cloth.

Look after a few days. You will see how the worms have mixed up the layers.

Worm charming

Worms come to the surface to breathe when it rains heavily, they might otherwise drown in water-logged soil.

If you bang on the lawn, worms may come up, thinking that it is raining.

WORM   ANT   EARWIG

MILLIPEDE

TICK

All kinds of different animals live in soil and rotting leaves, from minute ones which eat bacteria, to bigger ones such as earthworms and beetles.

SLUG

CENTIPEDE

Look in rotting leaves for some of these animals.

Do plants need soil?

Plants, like animals, cannot grow without food and water.

Green plants make the food they need through their leaves by using sunlight, but they also need soil for its minerals and nutrients. Soil also protects seeds from cold in the winter.

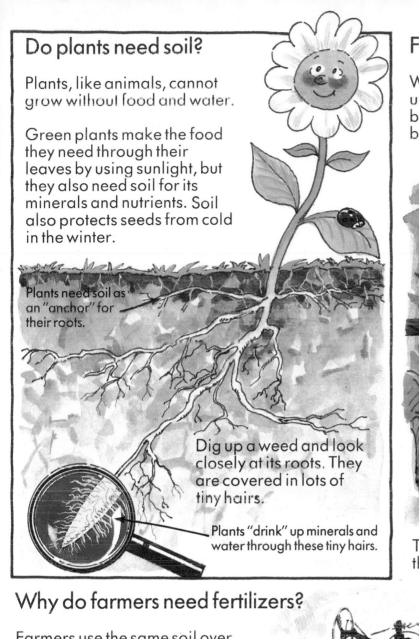

Plants need soil as an "anchor" for their roots.

Dig up a weed and look closely at its roots. They are covered in lots of tiny hairs.

Plants "drink" up minerals and water through these tiny hairs.

Feeding soil

Where plants, such as trees in jungles, grow undisturbed, their fallen leaves, fruits, and branches give the soil back minerals which have been taken up in the plant's roots.

The plants feed the soil, and the soil in turn feeds the plants.

Why do farmers need fertilizers?

Farmers use the same soil over and over again to grow crops which are then cut down and taken away. The soil becomes poorer and lacks the minerals that plants need.

Farmers add fertilizers to the soil which put back many of the lost minerals.

Animal manure is good for the soil too. Can you think why?

In the garden

Gardeners sometimes dig decayed plants, called compost, into the soil to replace the nutrients plants have taken out.

The inside of the heap gets warm as the bacteria rots the plants.

Compost heaps can be made in a corner of the garden with fruit skins, old vegetables, grass cuttings and other cut plants.

Surviving the cold

As summer weather cools in autumn, plants and animals in many parts of the world prepare for cold winter weather.

Mammals, including human beings and birds, are "warm-blooded". The food they eat acts like fuel to keep their bodies warm.

Some birds cannot find enough food during cold weather in the same place as they breed in summer.

You may see birds, such as swallows or martins, gathering on telephone wires at the end of summer. They fly south together to warmer places where they can find food. They return in the spring.

FLUFFED UP FEATHERS

In cold weather birds use their feathers to keep warm. Feathers trap a layer of air close to their bodies. They can fluff them up and tuck in their naked legs and beaks to keep warm.

Mammals have a coat of fur, wool or hair which helps to keep them warm. Furry animals can fluff up their fur in a similar way to a bird's feathers.

Air trapped in feathers and fur keeps birds and animals warm. Air is an insulator, which means it keeps in heat.

What are goose-pimples?

Muscles under the skin make fur and feathers stand on end. We have "goose-pimples" when we are cold which are made in the same way even though we have very little hair on our bodies.

You need clothes to keep your body warm. You will be warmer on a cold day with a few loose layers of clothes than one, thick layer. More layers trap more air.

About 20% of your body heat is lost through your head.

Blue with cold

Heat is carried around your body by your blood. When you are cold, blood vessels near the surface of your skin contract. This moves warm blood away from your skin so you lose less heat to the air.

You look blue or white because you have less red blood near the surface of your skin.

Extra underwear

Seals have thin fur, but an extra thick fat layer keeps them warm in icy seas.

Animals that live in places that are always cold, such as penguins in the Antarctic, have a thick layer of fat, called blubber, beneath their skins to keep them warm.

Deep sleep

Some animals, such as small rodents, cannot find enough food to eat in winter.

In the autumn it eats a lot while there is still plenty of food about. Its body builds up a layer of fat to feed off during the winter.

It finds a safe shelter and goes into a deep sleep until the weather warms up. This is called hibernation. When a mammal hibernates, its body temperature

falls well below normal and its breathing becomes slow and irregular. Its body works slowly, using the stored food.

Do plants die in winter?

Many plants die at the end of the summer.

Plants, such as poppies, cannot survive the cold weather. Their roots are not able to draw up water from frozen soil and their leaves and stems are damaged by frost.

The seeds fall through holes in the top of the pod and are blown away by the wind.

A poppy dies after it has produced seeds at the end of summer, but the plant survives in the form of seeds. The seeds which land on soil may grow into a new poppy in spring.

Why do some trees lose their leaves?

Trees lose water through their leaves. In summer this water is replaced by water drawn up through their roots.

Trees which lose their leaves in winter are called deciduous trees.

If the ground is cold or frozen, a tree's roots cannot draw up water. It sheds its leaves in autumn to stop it from losing all of its water.

BRANCH OF CONIFER

Some trees, called coniferous trees, keep most of their leaves in winter. They have small, tough, waxy leaves, which limits the amount of water they can lose.

Underground larder

Some plants, such as potatoes and daffodils, survive the winter underground with their own supply of food. The plants use the food store in spring for growing and flowering.

Daffodils store their food in bulbs. These contain buds which are ready to grow in spring.

Onions are also bulbs. Cut one in half and look for the small bud which is ready to sprout into a new plant.

When a potato plant dies down at the end of summer, it stores food in swollen stems – these are the potatoes. Each potato can produce a new plant in spring.

In the heat

In hot weather, plants lose a lot of water through their leaves. If this water is not replaced, they die.

Why is water necessary?

Plants need water to carry minerals up from the soil and for photosynthesis. Water also keeps the stems and leaves of non-woody plants rigid.

If you forget to water a plant it will droop. The plant will recover if you water it before it has died.

CELERY

COLOURED WATER

Water is drawn up through the plant's roots and travels up the stem to the leaves and flowers.

If you put a stick of celery in water coloured with food colouring, you can see that the water travels up the stem.

Prove that plants give off water

Cover a well-watered potted plant with a clear plastic bag. Tie it down around the pot so that air cannot get into the bag.

Put the plant in a sunny place.

After a few hours, the inside of the bag will be coated with drops of water.

Water comes out through tiny holes, called stomata, in the leaves. This loss of water is called transpiration.

MAGNIFIED LEAF

Extra protection

Plants grow well in jungles where it is hot and there is also a lot of rain.

In some parts of the world it is very hot but it hardly ever rains. Plants in these areas need to protect themselves from losing water.

A waxy skin helps to keep in the water.

Cacti store water in their thick stems. They can also store water in their roots. The roots spread over large areas or go down very deep to reach as much water as possible.

Cacti either have no leaves, or have tiny spines instead of leaves. They only have very few stomata on their stems.

The spines keep off thirsty animals.

On a hot day a tree can "drink" as much as 50 buckets of water through its roots. Most of this comes out invisibly through its leaves.

Keeping cool

Your body needs to stay at a temperature of about 98.6°F. If your body gets very hot, you could become ill.

You feel cooler in a breeze because sweat evaporates more quickly.

Fans do not cool the air but they help to cool you down by making a breeze.

Sweating is one of your body's ways of cooling. As the sweat dries up, or evaporates, it takes heat from your skin and cools you down.

Getting in a sweat

If you look at your palm or the skin inside your elbow through a magnifying glass, you can see tiny holes in the skin, called pores.

Sweat comes out through the pores.

Have you noticed how you look red and your veins stick out when you are hot?

Your blood is cooled by the air, which helps to cool down your body.

Blood vessels near the surface of your skin widen when you are hot so that more blood flows near the surface.

A waterproof skin

When you get wet, water drips off you because your skin is waterproof.

A drink helps to replace the water lost through sweating.

You lose sweat through your pores but your waterproof skin stops you losing too much.

Nearly three-quarters of your body is water. Water is needed to keep you alive and healthy.

How do animals keep cool?

Some animals, such as elephants, have very large ears. These are full of tiny blood vessels which are cooled in the air.

Slowly flapping its ears in the air helps to keep the elephant cool and comfortable.

If you see a dog resting after a run, it will probably be panting.

A dog cannot sweat. Instead water evaporates from its tongue and cools it down.

Food

Food gives your body the things it needs to heal cuts and scratches.

Food gives you energy to play and run about.

All animals, including you, need food. Food helps you to grow, to keep healthy and to give you the energy to run about, play games and lots of other things.

Some animals, such as cows, sheep and rabbits, only eat plants. They are called herbivores. Other animals, such as lions, cats and dogs, only eat meat. They are called carnivores. Others, including you, eat both plants and meat and are called omnivores.

Herbivores and carnivores

When you see herbivores, they always seem to be eating. But if you have a cat or dog, you will know it only has one or two meals a day.

A SHEEP EATS FOR ABOUT 20 HOURS A DAY

Why do herbivores eat more than carnivores? Which is more filling – a plateful of meat or a plateful of lettuce?

Plants contain a special substance called cellulose which is very tough. You cannot live on grass because your body cannot use the cellulose.

MAGNIFIED PLANT STEM

Lions rest while their bodies digest large meals.

Cows, and other herbivores, have special bacteria living in their stomachs which break the cellulose down into food their bodies can use. This is called digestion.

They need to eat a huge amount of plant food to get enough nourishment from it.

Meat is easy to digest and full of nourishment, so lions and other carnivores may only eat once every three days.

Your teeth

When you eat a mouthful of food, the first thing you do is to bite and chew it.

You have two main types of teeth. The sharp ones in front are for biting. They are called incisors and canines.

Your back teeth are for crushing and grinding up the food. They are called premolars and molars.

If you look at a cat's or dog's teeth, you will see that their canines are very long and pointed. Carnivores need those to rip up raw meat. Their premolars and molars are also sharper than yours.

FLAT, RIDGED TEETH

SHARP, POINTED CANINES

Horses are herbivores. Their teeth are flat and ridged for chewing grass and hay.

What do you eat?

You need to eat a variety of different kinds of foods because they do different jobs in your body. Some foods do more than one job.

MEAT · FISH · BEANS · EGGS

These foods contain protein. Proteins are the main body building foods and you need to eat a lot when you are growing.

You need protein, even when you are fully grown, because parts of your body wear out and need to be replaced.

When you rub yourself dry after a bath, you sometimes rub off dead skin. Dead skin is old skin cells. The protein you eat helps to build up new skin cells.

MILK · YOGHURT · CHEESE

These foods contain calcium which helps to make your bones and teeth strong. They also contain protein.

PASTA · RICE · BREAD · SUGAR

These foods are called carbohydrates. They give you most of your energy.

Soldiers and mountaineers usually carry a bar of chocolate for instant energy.

FRUIT · VEGETABLES

Fruits and vegetables contain some of the vitamins and minerals your body needs to keep it in good condition.

The cellulose, which your body cannot digest, makes the food your body cannot use bulky so that your muscles have something to push against when you go to the toilet.

OIL · MAYONNAISE · BUTTER · MARGARINE

Fats also give you energy and your body can use them as a store of emergency food.

Stored fat helps to keep you warm in cold weather.

APPLE · MILK · BREAD · BUTTER · POTATOES · GREEN BEANS · MEAT

Try to plan a meal, like the one here, using foods on this page or others you think of. It should contain everything you need to keep healthy.

Moving skeletons

Look around at living things. You will find that they all have a particular kind of shape.

Animals, such as cats, dogs, birds and you, have skeletons either on the inside or outside which give them shape.

Try making a giraffe out of clay. Can it stand up?

Your giraffe collapses because it has no frame, or skeleton, to support its body. If you put plastic straws in its legs and neck it will stand up.

STRAWS

How do you move?

Your skeleton is inside your body. It is made up of over 200 bones which are joined by tough fibres, called ligaments. The place where two bones meet is called a joint.

Your hips and shoulders have ball and socket joints so that you can move your legs and arms in most directions.

The lower part of your arm has two bones joined to your wrist bones. These make a pivot joint so that you can turn your hands over.

Your skull is made of bones which are fixed together and make a helmet of bone to protect your brain.

The ribs in your chest form a cage which protects your heart and lungs.

Your elbow joint works like a door hinge and can only move up and down.

Without joints you would not be able to bend or move. Your arms and legs are moved by muscles pulling on bones on either side of the joints.

Try to match some of the bones you can feel in your body with this skeleton.

Watch your muscles working

Hold one of your arms out straight and put your other hand just above the elbow, as shown in the picture.

BICEPS

Lift up the lower part of your arm. You will feel a muscle above your elbow, called the biceps, getting fat as it contracts.

The biceps becomes short as well as fat when it contracts and this pulls up the lower part of your arm.

When you lower your arm again, muscles at the back contract. The biceps is long and thin when your arm is straight.

Muscle strength

The more you use your muscles, the stronger they become.

Ask a friend to press his hands tightly together. Try to pull them apart by gripping each wrist and pulling outwards, as in the picture.

You will find it almost impossible to pull his hands apart because you do not use these muscles very often.

PULL

Try again by crossing your hands over and pushing his hands apart.

It is easy because you use pushing muscles often and they are strong.

PUSH

Outside skeletons

Insects, spiders, centipedes, millipedes and shell fish, such as crabs, all have their skeletons on the outside.

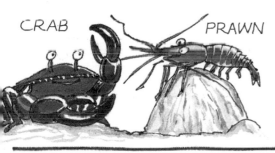

CRAB   PRAWN

LADYBIRD

TICK

If you look closely at a ladybird or a tick, you will find that the outside of its body is hard. This is because its skeleton, called the cuticle, is on the outside.

Its muscles are inside its body and limbs and are attached to the cuticle.

An outside skeleton gives these animals good protection against enemies.

PILL TICK

If you touch a pill tick it curls up and its whole body becomes a hard ball.

Animals without skeletons

Muscles cannot work unless they have something to push and pull against. Worms, caterpillars, slugs and snails have no skeleton, so how do they move?

The bodies of worms and caterpillars are supported by water pressure in their cells. Muscles use the edge of these cells to push and pull against.

The moving worm

Circular muscles contract—body becomes long and thin.

Front bristles grip.

Bristles grip the earth at back.

Back grip releases.

Muscles along body contract. Body becomes short and pulls the back forward.

Slugs and snails

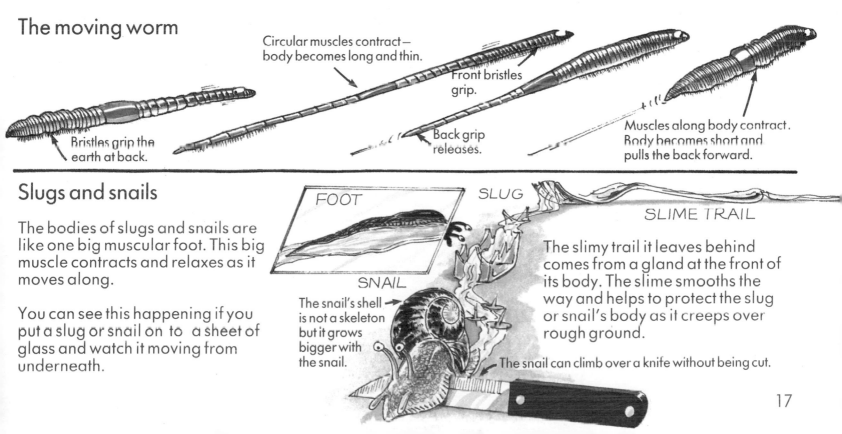

FOOT

SLUG

SLIME TRAIL

The bodies of slugs and snails are like one big muscular foot. This big muscle contracts and relaxes as it moves along.

You can see this happening if you put a slug or snail on to a sheet of glass and watch it moving from underneath.

SNAIL

The snail's shell is not a skeleton but it grows bigger with the snail.

The slimy trail it leaves behind comes from a gland at the front of its body. The slime smooths the way and helps to protect the slug or snail's body as it creeps over rough ground.

The snail can climb over a knife without being cut.

Unusual babies

Many baby animals, such as kittens and lambs, are exactly like their parents. But some babies, including caterpillars and tadpoles, look quite different from their parents. They go through a complete change, called metamorphosis, to become adults.

From caterpillars to butterflies

Butterflies mate early in spring, and the female then lays her tiny eggs on leaves.

EGGS

After a few days or weeks, tiny caterpillars hatch from the eggs. They eat part of the egg shell for their first meal, but soon move on to eat the leaves the eggs were laid on.

BUTTERFLIES MATING

CATERPILLAR HATCHES

The old skin splits and the caterpillar wriggles out in a new larger one.

Caterpillars spend their time eating and grow quickly. Their skins do not stretch and soon become too tight. They change their skins about four times as they grow.

Swimmers to hoppers

When the weather warms up in spring, male frogs go to their breeding ponds and sing in a croaky chorus to attract females. The male climbs on to the female's back, using special thumb-pads.

1

He is carried around on her back until the female frog lays her eggs, called spawn, which he then covers with sperms. The sperms swim through the egg jelly to fertilize the eggs.

SPAWN

2

3

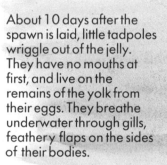

TADPOLE HATCHES

About 10 days after the spawn is laid, little tadpoles wriggle out of the jelly. They have no mouths at first, and live on the remains of the yolk from their eggs. They breathe underwater through gills, feathery flaps on the sides of their bodies.

4

FEATHER LIKE GILLS

After a day or two, their mouths develop and they start to eat tiny water plants, called algae.

When the caterpillar is fully grown, a few weeks after hatching, it stops eating and moves to a hidden twig or leaf. The caterpillar spins silk from its body to hold it firmly on the plant. It then sheds its skin, and changes into a pupa.

PUPA

The pupa becomes hard and looks like a broken twig or a bud, which helps to hide it from hungry birds. Inside, the caterpillar changes into a butterfly.

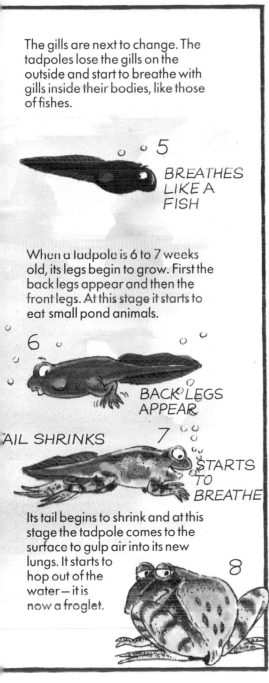

The gills are next to change. The tadpoles lose the gills on the outside and start to breathe with gills inside their bodies, like those of fishes.

5

BREATHES LIKE A FISH

When a tadpole is 6 to 7 weeks old, its legs begin to grow. First the back legs appear and then the front legs. At this stage it starts to eat small pond animals.

6

BACK LEGS APPEAR

TAIL SHRINKS

7

STARTS TO BREATHE

Its tail begins to shrink and at this stage the tadpole comes to the surface to gulp air into its new lungs. It starts to hop out of the water — it is now a froglet.

8

Watch them grow

If you have a cat, cover the dish with chicken wire to keep out playful paws.

You can collect frog spawn from ponds in a jar, and watch tadpoles change into frogs at home.

Transfer the eggs into a dish at home and cover them with pond water.

When the tadpoles start gulping air, put a brick into the dish to make a landing stage. As soon as the froglets start jumping out of the water, it is time to take them back to their pond.

Feed the tadpoles fresh pond plants until they grow legs, when they will need finely chopped raw meat.

If you take caterpillars or tadpoles home, keep a record in your biology scrapbook of the changes you see.

Keep them in your home

After two to three weeks the pupa skin splits and the adult butterfly pulls itself out.

At first its wings are wet and crumpled, but they stretch and dry after a couple of hours' rest.

The adult butterfly flies off to find food — nectar — a sugary substance from flowers. It also looks for a mate, and the life cycle starts again.

Look for caterpillars in summer on grasses and cabbages. Gently place a caterpillar in a large glass jar with some of the plant you found it on.

PUNCH AIR HOLES

RUBBER BAND

Cover the jar with some greaseproof paper held by a band. Punch some breathing holes in the paper with a needle. Keep the jar in a cool place, and feed the caterpillar fresh leaves of the same plant each day.

If you are lucky, you will see the caterpillar change into a butterfly. Take the butterfly back to where you found the caterpillar and watch it fly away.

Take care of living things. Only take them home if you can look after them properly.

From seed to seed

Most flowering plants grow from seeds.

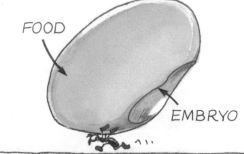

FOOD

EMBRYO

A seed is made of two parts, a food store and a baby plant, or embryo, which feeds on the food store.

The seed normally starts to grow in spring when the weather warms up and the soil is wet. The first part to grow is the root and then the shoot.

The seedling

The seedling lives off the food stored in its seed until it grows leaves. It then starts to make its own food by photosynthesis. It grows and produces flowers.

Sensitive roots

Roots are sensitive to gravity and always grow downwards.

Test a germinating bean to prove that this is true.

Soak a bean for 2 to 3 days, then pin it to a piece of cardboard or cork, resting on a damp cotton ball. Prop the card upright and wait for the root to grow.

PLACE PIN THROUGH THE FOOD STORE

CARDBOARD OR CORK, ABOUT 2½" x 2½".

As the root grows, turn the board as shown. Each time you turn the board the root will turn to grow downwards.

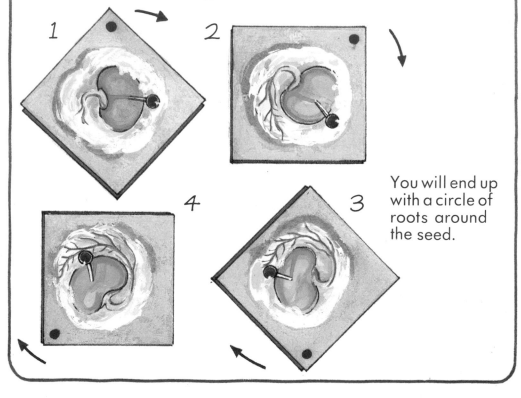

1

2

4

3

You will end up with a circle of roots around the seed.

Why do plants have flowers?

Flowers are the reproductive part of the plant. Without them plants could not produce seeds.

If you look closely at a buttercup or fuschia, you can see the male and female parts of the flower. Compare your flower with these pictures.

The ovary is the female part and is at the centre of the flower. The stigmas come out from the ovary and are easy to see.

BUTTERCUP

STAMENS

FUSCHIA

This is the male part, called the stamen. Its tip, called the anther, is covered in lots of tiny grains of pollen.

STIGMA

Before a flower can make new seeds, the stigma has to be fertilized by pollen. This is called pollination. The pollen usually comes from another plant of the same kind.

20

How does pollen travel?

Pollen is mainly carried from one plant to another by insects and the wind, but it is sometimes carried by birds, animals and water.

Pollen from the water lily is carried on the water to another flower.

Attracting insects

Flowers which are pollinated by insects usually produce sugary nectar to attract them. The plants also attract insects with their brightly coloured petals and sweet smells.

In spring and summer you can see bees, butterflies and other insects flying from flower to flower to feed on the nectar.

Try sucking the base of clover petals. The sweet taste is nectar.

CLOVER

While the insect eats, its body brushes against the stamen and pollen collects on its body.

When it visits another flower of the same kind, pollination will take place if the pollen brushes on to a ripe stigma.

Some petals have lines of colour leading to the centre of the flower to show the insect where to land.

PANSY

This flower has a special way of covering bees with pollen. When the bee lands, spring-like stamens flick up and cover the bee with pollen

You may have noticed that flowers, such as nicotiana and evening primrose smell strongly at night. This attracts moths to pollinate the flowers.

Blowing on the wind

Flowers which are pollinated by the wind need to produce lots of pollen to have a chance of reaching a stigma.

Try shaking a hazel catkin. The yellow dust that falls off is pollen.

This catkin is a male flower. The female catkin is feathery for catching pollen.

Grasses are wind pollinated. Pollen carried in the wind gives some people hayfever in summer.

Do wind pollinated flowers need to be colourful?

A new seed forms

When pollen lands on a stigma it grows a tube into the ovary to fertilize a female cell.

POLLEN

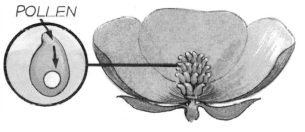

The petals wither and fall leaving ovaries, which are the fruit.

The seeds grow inside the fruits until they are ripe and ready to be scattered.

Travelling Seeds

All seeds grow inside fruits. Some of these fruits are the ones you eat, like apples and oranges, some are nuts, some are pods, some are berries and some are cones. Look carefully at the fruits and vegetables you eat and at plants growing in gardens and fields. You will see their seeds. Can you name the fruits around these pages?

When the fruit of a flowering plant is ripe, the seed or seeds in the fruit are scattered away from the parent plant. This gives some of them a better chance of finding the space, light and food they need to grow. Seeds are scattered in several different ways.

Hitch-hikers

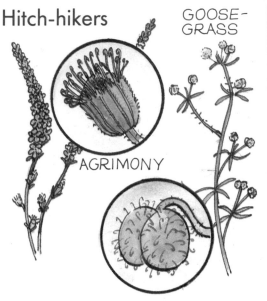

GOOSE-GRASS

AGRIMONY

Some seeds, such as burrs, "hitch" lifts from passing animals. The fruits are covered in lots of tiny hooks which can catch in the animal's fur. A burr can be carried a long way before it falls, or is scratched off.

15 M 10 M

You may catch burrs in your clothes.

Look closely at a burr. Can you see the tiny hooks?

Tasty fruits

Some seeds are inside soft, colourful fruits which are eaten by birds and animals.

The seeds are inside hard cases which pass out whole away from the parent plant in the droppings of the bird or animal.

Poppers

The pod is the fruit.

BEAN SEED

When seeds, such as beans, are fully grown, their pods burst open and flick the seeds away from the plant.

Under your feet

Some seeds fall to the ground and become sticky when wet. They stick to birds' and animals' feet and fall off again when they dry.

Try this experiment to see how many seeds you carry home after a summer country walk.

Fill a metal tray with soil.

Heat the soil in an oven to kill any seeds you may have dug up in the soil.

Scrape the mud from your shoes on to the soil, and water it well. Cover the tray with clear plastic and leave it in a warm place for 1 to 2 weeks. Do any seeds grow?

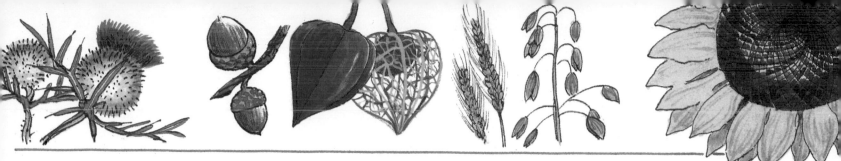

An unwelcome guest

Mistletoe grows on branches and trunks of trees. It sends its roots deep into the tree for water and minerals.

HOW DO SEEDS GET THERE?

Mistletoe seeds are very sticky. They stick to the bird's beak when it eats the berry. The bird later rubs its beak against a branch to wipe off the seeds.

The seeds lodge in the cracks of bark and, if conditions are right, another mistletoe will grow.

Ocean travellers

Coconuts may travel up to 1,200 miles on ocean currents before reaching land.

Fliers

Some seeds are blown by the wind to their new homes. Seeds which travel in this way normally have a special design which keeps them in the air for as long as possible.

Dandelion seeds are inside very small fruits, shaped like tiny parachutes. They can float on the wind for many miles before landing.

Blow a dandelion seed head. How far do the seeds go?

SEED

Another way seeds slow their fall from a tree is to spin like helicopter blades. You can make a paper model to see how this works.

1

Cut an oblong, about 8" × 2¾" from a piece of paper. make three cuts in it, as shown.

2   *3*

Fold over the two sides below the cuts, and bend the end up.

4

Fold out the two flaps at the top to make the blades.

Stand on a chair to drop your helicopter and watch it spin to the ground.

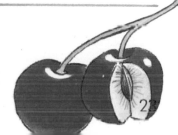

Sycamore seeds fall in this way, but they usually have only one blade.

SYCAMORE SEED

Cut off one of the blades from your paper helicopter. Does it still spin?

When you drop the one-bladed helicopter, you will find that it still spins. Try it out of doors and see how far it flies.

Trees

Trees are the largest living things on earth and they provide homes and food for many other plants and animals.

Is wood alive?

Snap a twig in half. Is it wet or dry? If the twig is alive, wet sap will ooze out.

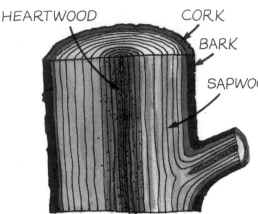

HEARTWOOD CORK BARK SAPWOOD

Inside the cork is a layer of wood which carries starch from the leaves to all parts of the tree. Inside this, a new layer of wood, called sapwood is being made each year. Sapwood carries water and minerals from the roots to the rest of the tree. In the middle of the trunk is old sapwood, called heartwood, which is dead.

A tree trunk is made of several types of wood and each has a job to do. The outside of the tree is protected by a layer of cork which is alive but its outside edge, bark, is dead.

The heartwood supports the tree but it can live without it.

How tall is a tree?

You can work out how tall a tree is quite easily with a pencil and the help of a friend.

Hold pencil at arm's length.

Walk back until the pencil appears the same height as tree.

Turn the pencil on its side, bottom edge against tree.

STOP!

Ask a friend to walk away to one side of the tree, like this. Shout "stop" when she reaches the end of the pencil.

Measure from your friend to the tree with a tape measure. This distance is the height of the tree.

Bark rubbings

A tree's bark cracks, splits or peels as the tree grows and its pattern is different for each kind of tree.

Hold the paper steady, or tie it top and bottom.

Rub a crayon firmly over paper.

Bark
Acorn
Oak Apple
Twig
Leaf
Oak Tree

Try making posters of different kinds of trees. Add twigs, fruits, flowers and leaf rubbings or prints. You can find out how to make prints on pages 36-37.

You can make bark rubbings, as shown above, and glue them on to a large sheet of paper to make a tree poster.

How old is a tree?

A tree makes a new ring of wood each year.

If you come across an old tree stump, you can find out how old the tree was by counting the number of rings.

Never carve your name on a tree. Disease may enter the wound and kill the tree.

Life in a tree

Look at a tree near your home. How many different plants and animals live in, on and under it? What do they eat?

This oak tree shows some of the living things you may find.

Crows and other birds build nests high in the branches.

CROWS

MALE FLOWER

Oak apples are made by female gall wasps who lay eggs in an oak shoot. The tree swells up around the eggs making round balls, called galls. The wasp larvae eat the galls when they hatch. Spangle galls are also made this way.

OAK APPLE

ACORN

SPANGLE GALLS

The woodpecker uses its beak to drill holes in dead wood to find insects to eat. It may drill out a nesting hole where a branch has broken off and the wood is softer.

Look closely at bark for hidden insects.

EARWIG

NUTHATCH

Caterpillars and other larvae eat the leaves.

MILLIPEDE

TICK

Leaf Miners chew tunnels through the leaves.

Upsidedown, the nuthatch searches for insects. It also eats acorns, which it wedges in a crack and hammers open with its bill.

Squirrels build nests of leaves and twigs, called dreys, in the forks of branches.

Mosses grow in damp shady places and do not have proper roots. Ferns can live on the trunk of the tree where their roots grip on to the mosses.

Ivy climbs the tree towards the sunlight. Many insects live on its leaves and stems.

MOSS

Squirrels eat bird's eggs, young birds and acorns. They often bury extra acorns for winter food. If forgotten, the acorn may grow into a new oak tree.

Bracket fungus grows where the bark is broken. It may rot the wood and kill the tree.

Toadstools grow in dead leaves.

Foxes may live in a hole, called an earth, which they dig under the roots of the tree. They hunt at night for small animals and birds.

Primroses and bluebells flower in spring before the leaves take away all the light.

Flight design

Wherever you are, you will see birds. They live in towns, in the country, on the seashore and even in deserts.

With the help of wings, birds can build nests and find food in many places that other animals cannot reach. See page 35 for ways of feeding birds at home.

Feathers

All birds have feathers and most, except birds such as ostriches and penguins, can fly. Feathers help birds to fly and keep them warm and waterproof.

Even the smallest hummingbird has about 1,000 feathers.

Feathers are made of the same material as your hair and nails, which is called keratin.

Soft, fluffy feathers, called down, keep the bird warm.

NAILS

HAIR

Like hair and nails, feathers can be soft or hard.

The outer wing and body feathers are stiff but very light.

Each little strand of the feather is joined by tiny overlapping hooks.

Cleaning and preening

STROKE UP TO TIP OF FEATHER

You can push the hooks apart with a finger. If you then stroke along the feather they will close again, like a zipper.

Birds use their beaks to "zip" ruffled feathers together. This is called preening.

When a water bird preens, it usually spreads oil from a gland near its tail over the feathers to make them waterproof.

Birds need to keep their feathers clean and tidy to fly and keep warm. They often bath in water or dust before preening.

When oil is spilt from an oil tanker, many sea birds are covered with it. The heavy oil sticks their feathers together and they cannot fly. They try to clean themselves but they swallow the oil which poisons them and they die.

Using the air

Drop two pieces of paper, one crumpled and one flat, at the same time and from the same height. Which piece lands first?

The flat piece falls more slowly. This is because it has a larger area supported by the air than the paper ball. This is called air resistance.

When a bird's wings are stretched out to fly, they cover a large area. Air resistance helps to keep the bird in the air.

Bones are very heavy, but birds have hollow bones which help to make them light.

A wing is made of overlapping feathers joined to bones. When the wing flaps down, the feathers overlap and press against the air. When the wing comes up, muscles separate the feathers letting air through.

You can try this with water. Push your hands through it with your fingers together and then with them apart.

The greater push you feel when your fingers are together is like a wing as it flaps down.

Designed for flying

A bird's wing has a curved, streamlined shape which is thicker at the front and thins down towards the back. This shape is

Air is pushed apart by the wing.

LOW PRESSURE

The air above has further to go to reach the back of the wing and so moves faster.

HIGH PRESSURE

called an airfoil. When air meets the wing it moves in the way shown above.

Fast moving air has less pressure than slow or still air. This means that there is more air pressure below the wing than above and this pushes, or lifts, the wing upwards.

Try this test to show how air pressure works.

LOW PRESSURE

AIR PUSHES UP

Hold one end of a small strip of paper against your chin. Blow straight ahead. The paper lifts because the air pressure on top is less than the pressure underneath.

Take off

A bird's body has to be strong and very light to fly.

A bird needs speed for take off so that its wings will lift it into the air. Some run, others jump into the air and some push off from the water.

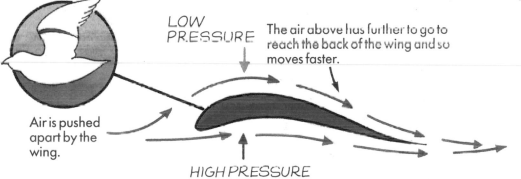

Birds nesting in trees and on cliffs take off by falling into the air.

A mallard pushes down hard with its webbed feet to leap up from the water.

A swan has heavy wings and needs to run quickly along the surface of the water, flapping hard, to take off.

Ponds and fishes

If you live near a pond, ask an adult to explore it with you and see how many different plants and animals you can find. A few of them are shown in this picture.

Be careful not to fall in!

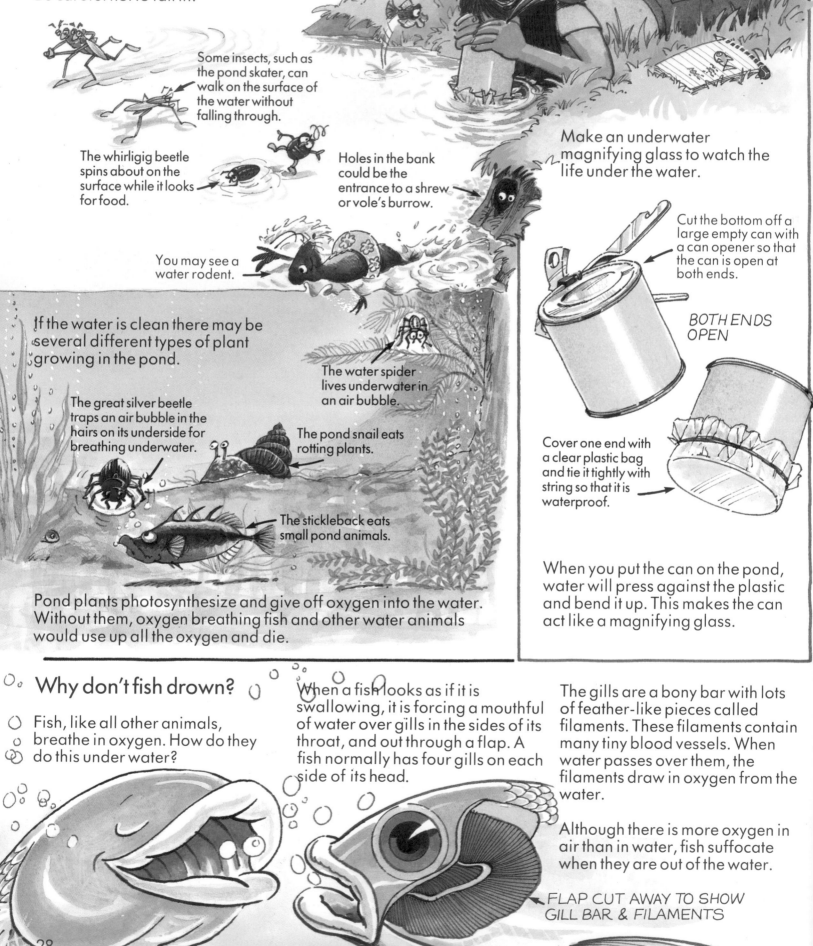

Some insects, such as the pond skater, can walk on the surface of the water without falling through.

The whirligig beetle spins about on the surface while it looks for food.

You may see a water rodent.

Holes in the bank could be the entrance to a shrew or vole's burrow.

Make an underwater magnifying glass to watch the life under the water.

Cut the bottom off a large empty can with a can opener so that the can is open at both ends.

BOTH ENDS OPEN

Cover one end with a clear plastic bag and tie it tightly with string so that it is waterproof.

If the water is clean there may be several different types of plant growing in the pond.

The great silver beetle traps an air bubble in the hairs on its underside for breathing underwater.

The water spider lives underwater in an air bubble.

The pond snail eats rotting plants.

The stickleback eats small pond animals.

Pond plants photosynthesize and give off oxygen into the water. Without them, oxygen breathing fish and other water animals would use up all the oxygen and die.

When you put the can on the pond, water will press against the plastic and bend it up. This makes the can act like a magnifying glass.

Why don't fish drown?

Fish, like all other animals, breathe in oxygen. How do they do this under water?

When a fish looks as if it is swallowing, it is forcing a mouthful of water over gills in the sides of its throat, and out through a flap. A fish normally has four gills on each side of its head.

The gills are a bony bar with lots of feather-like pieces called filaments. These filaments contain many tiny blood vessels. When water passes over them, the filaments draw in oxygen from the water.

Although there is more oxygen in air than in water, fish suffocate when they are out of the water.

FLAP CUT AWAY TO SHOW GILL BAR & FILAMENTS

Is shape important?

Water is 800 times denser than air. This is why it is much harder to walk through water than to walk on land. Fish need streamlined shapes to be able to swim quickly through the water.

WATER FLOWS EASILY PAST THE FISH

Upstairs, downstairs

A fish can float at different levels in the water by blowing up or letting down a bag of gas, called a swim bladder, under its spine.

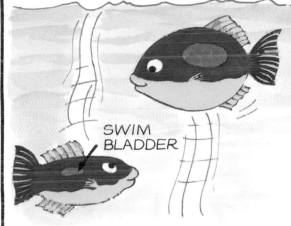

SWIM BLADDER

Without a swim bladder, the fish would sink when it stopped swimming.

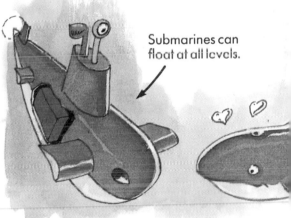

Submarines can float at all levels.

Which shape wins?

Cut out two small plastic boats from an old plastic bottle, like this.

Make one boat shaped and the other square, both with notches at the back, as shown.

Squeeze a blob of dishwashing liquid over the notches. Put them in a bathful of water next to each other. Watch what happens.

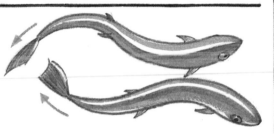

The dishwashing liquid acts like fuel to power the boats.

The square boat is slower because water cannot stream past it. The shape of real boats are copied from fish.

Expert swimmers

Fish have bendy spines which run along the whole length of their bodies.

Muscles pull on each side of a fish's spine in turn. This causes a wave-like movement to go down its body which pushes it through the water.

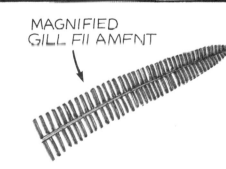

Its tail acts as both a paddle and rudder and its fins help it to balance, steer and stop.

A submarine is built like a fish. It has ballast tanks which are filled with water to make it sink and are pumped full of air to make it float upwards.

What does a submarine's shape remind you of?

If you put a small paintbrush in water, its bristles fluff out. When you take it out, they close up.

MAGNIFIED GILL FILAMENT

This is what happens to its gill filaments when a fish is taken out of the water. The filaments stick together and the blood vessels are less able to draw in air.

You can watch pond animals at home. See page 36 for details of how to make an aquarium.

Animal senses – 1

Sight, hearing, smell, taste and touch are all senses which tell you a lot about what is going on around you. Without them you would not know if you are hot or cold, comfortable or in danger. Your eyes are like cameras which take pictures of the world.

This picture shows you the parts of an eyeball.

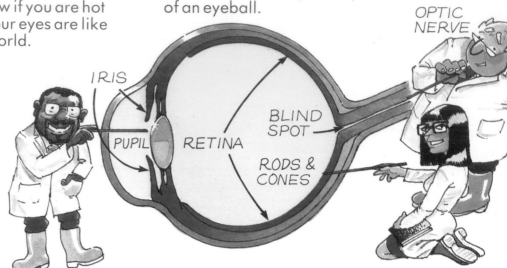

IRIS

PUPIL   RETINA

BLIND SPOT

RODS & CONES

OPTIC NERVE

Eyes need light to work. When you look at this book, light bounces off it and into your eye through the black hole in the middle, called the pupil.

The light touches special cells at the back of your eyeball and the information is sent to your brain by a nerve, called the optic nerve. Your brain then receives the information your eyes are taking

in. Too much light can damage these special cells. The coloured ring around your pupil, called the iris, closes up in bright light, making the pupil smaller. It opens up in dim light.

Watch your pupils close.

Look in a mirror in a dim room. Watch one eye and shine a torch into that eye. What happens to the size of the pupil? Does it change when you turn off the torch?

Why can't you see colour at night?

You have two types of cells at the back of your eye, called rods and cones. Cones only work in bright light and they pick up colours. In the dark there is not enough light

bouncing off things for the cones to work. You "see" instead with the rods which can work in dim light but do not pick up colour.

Night sight

Cats and other night hunters have mostly rod cells in their eyes. They can see much better in the dark than you can.

During the day, a cat's pupils are narrow slits but at night they open to catch as much light as possible.

DAY

NIGHT

Do carrots help you see in the dark?

Your rod cells need vitamin A to keep healthy. Carrots contain carotene which is related to vitamin A. Healthy eyes are better at seeing in the dark.

Invisible colours

An evening primrose looks all one colour to you but it looks quite different to a bee. A bee's eyes can see another sort of light, called ultra violet light, which is invisible to you. Many flowers have markings which can be seen in ultra violet light and they guide bees to nectar at the centre of the flower.

YOU SEE THIS

BEES SEE THIS

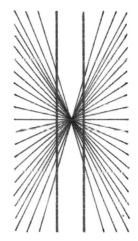

Can you see behind you?

Your eyes are on the front of your head but some animals, like rabbits and deer, have their eyes on the sides of their heads.

Look straight ahead with your arms behind your back. Bring your arms slowly forward until you can see both hands. The area in front of your two hands is called your "field of vision".

You cannot see any further back because of where your eyes are.

A hare can see behind as well as in front of its body because its eyes are on the side. This helps it to spot an enemy creeping up from behind.

HARE

Animals with eyes on the sides of their heads see most things with one eye at a time. You see things with two eyes which helps you know exactly where they are. Prove this to yourself by trying this test.

Try touching the corner of a table with a pencil – it is easy. Then try to touch the same corner with one eye closed. Can you do it?

Hunting animals have eyes in the front for pouncing accurately.

Can you believe your eyes?

Are these two red lines straight? After looking at them, put a ruler against the lines to find out.

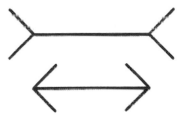

Which of these two lines is longer? Again, you can measure them after looking to find out the answer.

These tests help to show you that it is your brain which "sees" the pictures, rather than your eyes.

What is your blind spot?

Hold this page at arm's length, close your left eye. Look at the square and slowly bring it towards you. When the circle disappears you have found your blind spot.

Try again, closing your right eye and look at the circle instead of the square.

You have a blind spot in each eye where the optic nerve joins the retina and there are no rods and cones.

31

Animal senses – 2

How do you hear noises?

Throw a stone into a pond or lake and watch the waves spread out in bigger and bigger circles. Anything floating on the water will bob on the waves but will not move along. The waves move through the water but it stays still.

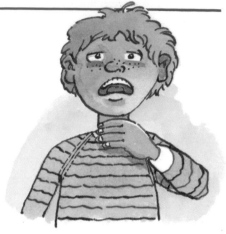

This is what happens to noises in the air. A noise makes waves in the air, called vibrations.

You can hear more clearly if you cup your hands behind your ears.

Your ears pick up the vibrations and send information about the noise to your brain.

Try talking to a friend about 30 long steps away. Don't shout. Can he hear you? Try again using a homemade telephone like the one on this page.

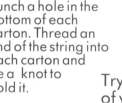

To make the telephone you need two empty yoghurt cartons and a long piece of string.

Punch a hole in the bottom of each carton. Thread an end of the string into each carton and tie a knot to hold it.

Your friend can hear you now because vibrations from your voice are carried along the string to his yoghurt carton.

Try putting your fingers on the front of your neck when you talk in a deep voice. You can feel it vibrating. In your neck is your voice box and as it vibrates it makes a noise.

Where is the noise?

Many animals have ears which can move round to "face" a noise. Look at the donkey's ears in these pictures. First it hears one car. What happens when it hears two noises? If you have a cat or dog, you can see it prick up its ears when it hears something.

You may be able to wiggle your ears a little, but you cannot move them around like a donkey.

You know where a noise is coming from because you hear it in one ear before the other. You can test this with a friend.

Blindfold your friend and cover one of her ears. Tap a can in front, behind and on each side of her. Does she know where you are? Try again with both of her ears uncovered. Is she more accurate this time?

Silent noises?

Some animals can hear sounds which you cannot hear. You can buy a "silent" whistle for your dog which makes a very high note. The dog hears it but you cannot.

Animals, such as barn owls, which hunt at night have much better hearing than you. They use their ears, as well as their eyes, to track down food in the dark.

Touch

When you pick up a pencil, you feel it because of cells in your skin which are sensitive to touch. These cells tell you about hot, cold, rough and smooth things.

If you put your hand on something sharp, the pain you feel makes you pull your hand away instantly. Pain acts like an alarm signal to warn your body when it is in danger.

Some parts of your body are more sensitive to touch than others. Try this test to find out where your sense of touch works best.

Ask a friend to close her eyes. Lightly press one wooden match and then two, held about 1/8" apart, on her back. Can she tell whether there are one or two matches? Try again on her wrist, arm and fingertips.

You will find that her finger tips are best at telling the difference. Why do you think they are more sensitive?

Whiskers

A cat's whiskers act like a fan of "feelers" around its head. At night it uses them to feel things in its way.

Smell

When you sniff, you draw smells up inside your nose where there are smell sensitive cells. These send information about the smell to your brain.

Smell can warn you that toast is burning or that food is bad as well as telling you that something delicious is cooking.

You may have noticed that you cannot taste food when you have a cold and a blocked nose. You taste with your tongue but your sense of taste is very weak without smell.

Many animals use smell to find food as well as for recognizing mates and enemies.

A mole is nearly blind and uses smell to find worms in the soil.

Most dogs have poor eyesight but they have 25 times more smell sensitive cells than you.

Insects do not have noses to smell with. Moths smell with their antennae. A male gypsy moth can smell a mate as far as 7 miles away.

A house fly tastes with its feet.

ANTENNAE

Attracting living things

Wherever you live, in the town or in the country, there are many ways of encouraging living things to visit you.

Wild patch

Most wild creatures do not like neat, tidy gardens. Ask your parents if you can have a corner of your garden to turn into a wild patch.

LONG GRASS

HONEYSUCKLE

BIRDS FEEDING ON INSECTS

COMPOST HEAP

A pile of rotting wood can make a home for insects.

In your wild patch, leave the grass to grow long and let wild flowers grow undisturbed.

This would be a good place to build a compost heap (see page 9). Birds will come to eat the insects that live in it.

If wild flowers do not grow in your patch, you can sow your own wild flower seeds. You can buy the seeds in a garden shop, or have fun collecting them for yourself.

DUG OVER PATCH

COW PARSLEY

POPPY

BUTTERCUP

DANDELION

FORGET-ME-NOT

You can collect wild flower seeds throughout late spring and summer after the plants have flowered. Look for wild flowers on waste land in towns and on the edges of lanes and fields in the country.

Take a bag for your seeds and shake the heads of flowers into it.

Clear some small patches, about 12 in. × 12 in. square, in your wild patch. Dig the soil over and plant the seeds about ½ - ¾ in. deep. Water them well.

The grass will soon grow again, and next spring and summer your wild patch should be full of wild flowers.

If you do not have a garden, you can plant wild flower seeds in a windowbox.

Make sure your box is safe and cannot fall off the ledge.

Butterfly guests

Butterflies will visit the wild flowers in your wild patch. They feed on flowers which have lots of nectar – you may have some in your garden.

Homemade butterfly flower

You can make your own flower to attract butterflies.

Fill a small bottle with honey dissolved in water. Soak some cotton in the mixture and use it to plug the top. Fix the bottle to the top of a stick with rubber bands and push the bottom into the ground.

A purple paper collar, held on with a rubber band, helps to attract butterflies.

Night visitors

If you put a light by a window on a summer night, several different kinds of moth will come to the window which you can watch from inside.

Window display

If you put food out on your windowsill, birds will soon come and eat, even if you are watching from inside.

Ask an adult to wedge a stick across the window. You can hang food from it as well as putting food on the sill.

Some food ideas:

Many supermarkets sell shelled nuts and fruit in net bags. You can fill an old net bag with nuts and tie it on to your stick.

Thread string through peanuts in their shells to hang up.

Make a small hole in the base of a yoghurt carton and thread some string through with a wooden match tied to the end to hold it. Fill the carton with a mixture of melted lard, breadcrumbs and currants. Let it harden before hanging it up.

Make a note of the different birds that come and the food that they like best.

PEANUTS

YOGHURT CARTON MIXTURE

HALF COCONUT

NUTS

Greenfinches, tits and sparrows will eat the hanging food.

Birds, such as blackbirds, will take food from the sill.

Bird bath

Birds need water to drink as well as for bathing.

You can make a very simple bird bath from a garbage can lid placed on bricks. Keep it filled with clean water.

In winter, melt any ice with a kettle of hot water in the morning, or keep a night light burning under the lid.

If you have a cat, only attract birds to places out of its reach.

35

Collecting things

Keep a record of the things you see, as well as your experiments, in your biology scrapbook. You can add pressed flowers, leaf prints, sprays or rubbings, feathers and your drawings.

If you keep your scrapbook up-to-date, it will be an interesting record of living things throughout the year.

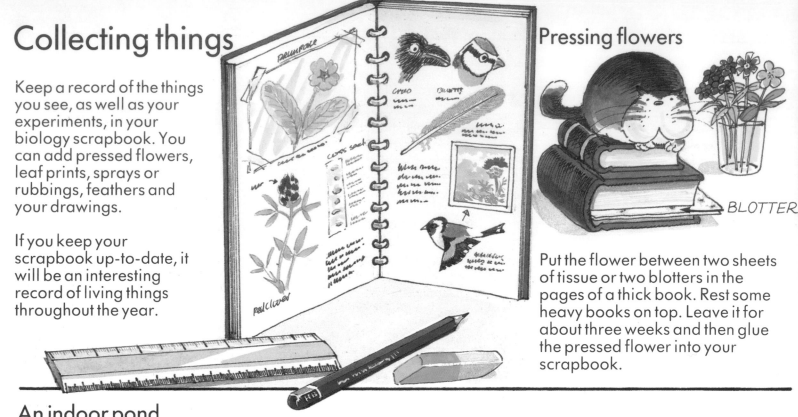

Pressing flowers

BLOTTER

Put the flower between two sheets of tissue or two blotters in the pages of a thick book. Rest some heavy books on top. Leave it for about three weeks and then glue the pressed flower into your scrapbook.

An indoor pond

You can turn a glass tank into a lively pond at home.

Collect gravel from a stream or buy it in a pet shop. Clean it thoroughly in running water and then put it in the tank. Add some clean, hard stones to keep the gravel steady.

Ram's-horn snails are good "cleaners". They eat the green algae which grows at the side of the tank.

Keep sticklebacks in the tank. They eat water fleas and other small water animals. Buy some extra food from a pet shop to feed them.

In spring, the male stickleback's belly becomes bright red. He builds a nest. When he sees a female stickleback, fat with eggs, he does a zigzag dance to invite her to the nest and they mate.

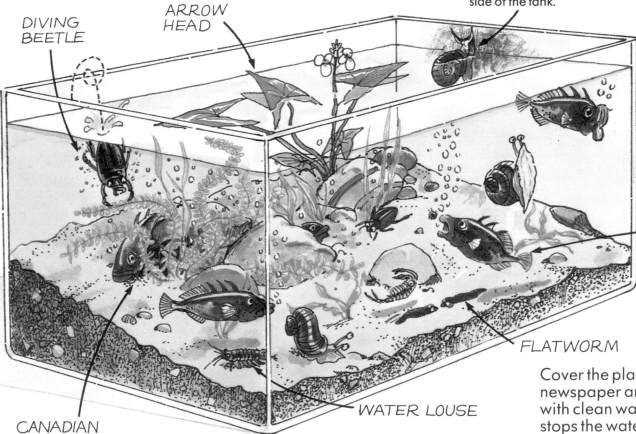

DIVING BEETLE

ARROW HEAD

STICKLEBACK

Collect or buy roundworms, flatworms, freshwater lice, shrimps, water fleas and water beetles.

FLATWORM

CANADIAN POND WEED

WATER LOUSE

Slope the gravel forwards so that dirt collects at the front.

Pond animals need oxygen, so put in some Canadian pondweed and arrowhead. Push the roots or the bases of their stems into the gravel.

Cover the plants with a sheet of newspaper and gently fill the tank with clean water. The newspaper stops the water disturbing the gravel and plants. Take it out when the tank is full. Leave the tank for a week before adding animals. Do not stand it in the sunlight or too much algae will grow.

Leaf rubbings

You can make attractive leaf rubbings of dry autumn leaves.

Cover the leaf with paper and rub all over the leaf with a crayon. Press hard at the edges and down the veins so that they stand out.

Leaf prints

Put a leaf face down on some newspaper and dab shoe polish gently on the back like this.

Place the leaf, polish side down, on to a sheet of paper with a blotter on top. Rub over the leaf, then lift off the blotter and the leaf.

Leaf sprays

Make your leaf spray out of doors. Put the leaf on some paper and rest it on newspaper. Use a can of spray paint to spray over the leaf – make sure you go over the edges. Leave the paint to dry before removing the leaf.

The country code

Keep to these simple rules when you go into the country. You can enjoy looking at plants and animals without disturbing or harming them.

KEEP YOUR DOG ON A LEASH

DON'T LITTER

CLOSE GATES BEHIND YOU

PROTECT ALL WILDLIFE

Don't break branches off trees.

Plastic bags can kill cows and sheep if they swallow them. Bottles and cans may cut their feet.

Put your litter in a can or take it home with you.

Don't throw things into ponds and streams or you may pollute the water.

If you cannot open a gate, climb over at the hinge end where it is strongest.

Don't damage fences, hedges and walls by climbing over them.

KEEP TO FOOTPATHS

Stay on footpaths or you may damage crops or disturb wildlife.

If you find a bird's nest, do not disturb it or take any eggs. You can take home empty egg shells you find on the ground.

If you pick wild flowers to press, only take one or two. You cannot dig up wild flower plants without the owner's permission. There are some wildflowers which you must not pick. You can get a list of these from your local nature reserve.

Small animals can climb into bottles and not be able to get out again.

DON'T LIGHT FIRES

Hay, heath and bracken catch fire easily so be careful with matches.

If you discover a fire, tell an adult immediately and the fire department.

Glossary

carbon dioxide This is a gas. When you breathe in air, your body uses the oxygen in the air and makes carbon dioxide which you breathe out. Plants take carbon dioxide from the air and use it for photosynthesis.

carnivore An animal which eats only meat.

cellulose The tough walls of plant cells, sometimes called fibre.

chlorophyll The green chemical in the leaves and stems of plants which takes in energy from sunlight.

coniferous trees Trees which keep their leaves during the winter. They lose a few leaves at a time throughout the year.

deciduous trees Trees which lose all their leaves in autumn.

fertilization When a male cell joins a female cell and a new animal or plant is made.

field of vision The area you can see around you while you are looking straight ahead

germination This is when a seed begins to grow. A seed needs warmth, water and oxygen to sprout.

gill The organ a fish has on each side of its throat for breathing under water.

An animal which eats only plants.

metamorphosis The complete change some baby animals go through to become adults, e.g. tadpole to a frog.

nectar The sugary liquid made by some flowers to attract insects.

omnivore An animal which eats both meat and plants.

oxygen A gas in the air which is used by your body when you breathe in. It is made by plants during photosynthesis.

photosynthesis The way plants make sugar and starch from carbon dioxide, sunlight and water by using chlorophyll.

pollination When pollen leaves one flower's stamen and is carried to the stigma of another flower.

senses Sight, hearing, smell, touch and taste are all senses and their job is to tell your body about your surroundings.

swim bladder A bag of gas under a fish's spine which it can blow up or let down to float at different levels in the water without any effort.

transpiration This is when plants lose tiny, invisible droplets of water, mainly through their leaves, into the air.

warm-blooded An animal who can keep the same body temperature whatever the temperature is around it.